Let Us
Pray

LET
US
PRAY

WATCHMAN NEE

Translated from the Chinese

Christian Fellowship Publishers, Inc.
New York

Available from the Publishers at:

11515 Allecingie Parkway
Richmond, Virginia 23235

TRANSLATOR'S PREFACE

What is prayer? Are we really praying when we pray? Do we know the power of prayer? These matters and others must be understood if we would have a real prayer life and be effective in prayer.

In this little volume of collected messages given over a long period of ministry by the author, and which are now translated and published in English for the first time, Watchman Nee shares with us the lessons on prayer that he has learned through the years.* He considers prayer to be a mystery, though not something that is incomprehensible. He views prayer as the greatest work to which men are called. It is a working together with God. Through it, God's purpose is accomplished and Satan's intentions are broken. And its benefit to the one who prays is something great as well.

Let us therefore follow the admonition of our blessed Lord, who said: "Rise and pray" (Luke 22.46).

---

* It should be noted that whereas this volume chiefly presents the general principles of prayer, more specific treatment on corporate prayer can be found in another of Mr. Nee's works: *The Prayer Ministry of the Church* (New York, Christian Fellowship Publishers, 1973), translated from the Chinese.

CONTENTS

1 | What Is Prayer?

Prayer is the most wonderful act in the spiritual realm as well as a most mysterious affair.

Prayer: a Mystery

Prayer is a mystery; and after we have considered a few questions on the subject I believe we will appreciate even more the mysterious character that surrounds prayer—for these are questions quite difficult to answer. Yet this observation is not meant to suggest that the mystery of prayer is incomprehensible or that the various problems concerning prayer are inexplicable. It is merely indicative of the fact that few people really know very much about them. In view of this, few are truly able to accomplish much for God in prayer. The power of prayer lies not in how much we pray but in how much our prayers are in accordance with the principle of prayer. Only prayers of this kind are of true value.

The foremost question to be asked is, Why pray? What is the use of praying? Is not God omniscient as well as omnipotent? Why must He wait till we pray before He commences to work? Since He knows, why must we tell Him everything (Phil. 4.6)? Being almighty, why does God not work directly? Why should He need our prayers? Why is it that only those who ask are given, only those who seek find, and only those who knock enter in (Matt. 7.7)? Why does God say: "Ye have not, because ye ask not" (James 4.2)?

Upon asking the above questions we must then continue to inquire as follows: Is prayer contrary to the will of God? What is the relationship between prayer and righteousness?

We know God never does anything against His own will. If opening doors is God's will, why should He wait until we knock before He opens? Why does He not simply open for us according to His own will without requiring us to knock? Being omniscient, God knows we need to have doors opened; why, then, must He wait for our knocking before He opens? If the door is to be opened and if opening doors is in accordance with God's will, and if furthermore He also knows that we need it to be opened, why does He wait for us to knock? Why does He not just open the door? What advantage does our knocking give to God?

Yet we must further ask these questions: Since God's will is to open the door and since opening the door is in accord with righteousness, will God nevertheless open the door if we do *not* knock? Or would He rather have His will and righteousness delayed without accomplishment in order to wait for our prayers? Will He really allow His will of opening doors to be restrained by our not knocking?

If so, will not the will of God be limited by us? Is God really almighty? If He is almighty, why can He not open the door all by himself—why instead must He wait till we knock? Is God really able to accomplish His own will? But if He truly is able, then why is His opening of doors (God's will) governed by our knocking (man's prayer)?

By asking all these questions we come to realize that prayer *is* a great mystery. For here we see a principle of God's working, which is, that God's people must pray before God himself will rise up and work: His will is only to be realized through the prayers of those who belong to Him: the prayers of the believers are to accomplish His will: God will not fulfill His will alone—He will perform only after His people show their sympathy in prayers.

Such being the case, it can therefore be said that prayer is none other than an act of the believer working together with God. Prayer is the union of the believer's thought with the will of God. The prayer which a believer utters on earth is but the voicing of the Lord's will in heaven. Prayer is not the expressing of our wish for God to yield to our petition and fill up our selfish desire. It is not a forcing of the Lord to change His will and perform what He is unwilling to do. No, prayer is simply speaking out the will of God through the mouth of the believer. Before God, the believer asks in prayer for the Lord's will to be done.

Prayer does not alter that which God has determined. It never changes anything; it merely achieves what He has already foreordained. Prayerlessness, though, *does* effect a change, because God will let many of His resolutions go suspended due to the lack from His people of prayerful cooperation with Him.

"Verily I say unto you, What things soever ye shall bind on earth shall be bound in heaven; and what things soever ye shall loose on earth shall be loosed in heaven" (Matt. 18.18). We are most familiar with this word of our Lord, yet it should be realized that this word has reference to prayer. And it is immediately followed by this statement of Christ's: "Again I say unto you, that if two of you shall agree on earth as touching anything that they shall ask, it shall be done for them of my Father who is in heaven" (v.19).

Heaven Governed by Earth

Here is clearly stated the relationship between prayer and God's work. God in heaven will only bind and loose what His children on earth have bound and loosed. Many things there are which need to be bound, but God will not bind them by himself alone. He wants His people to bind them on earth first, and then He will bind them in heaven. Many things are there also which should be loosed; but again, God is not willing to loose them alone: He waits until His people loose them on earth and then He will loose them in heaven. Think of it! All the actions in heaven are governed by the actions on earth! And likewise, all the movements in heaven are restricted by the movements on earth! God takes great delight in putting all His own works under the control of His people. (Yet it should be pointed out that these words in Matthew are not spoken to carnal people, for such are not qualified to hear them. Let us be very careful here lest the flesh come in, for in that case we shall offend God in many respects.)

There is one passage in Isaiah which conveys the same thought as is found here in Matthew: "Thus saith Jehovah, the Holy One of Israel, and his Maker: Ask me of the things that are to come; concerning my sons, and concerning the work of my hands, command ye me" (45.11). As we consider this word may we truly be pious, allowing no flesh to come in stealthily. God desires humble men such as we to command Him! He commences to do His work at our command! Whatever action God may take in heaven, be it binding or loosing, it is all done according to the command we give on earth.

Earth must bind first before heaven will bind; earth must loose first before heaven will loose. God never does anything against His will. It is not because the earth has bound something that the Lord is then forced to bind that which He has not wished to bind. Not so. He binds in heaven what has been bound on earth simply because His original will has always been to bind what the earth has eventually bound. He waits till His people on earth bind what heaven has aspired to bind, and then He will hearken to their command and bind for them what they have asked. The very

fact that God is willing to hear the command of His
people and bind what they have bound is evidence that
He has already willed to so bind (for all the wills of
God are eternal). Why does He not bind earlier?
Since it is His will to bind, and His will is eternal, why
does He not bind sooner what should be bound according to His own will? Why must He wait for the
earth to bind before He will bind in heaven? Is it true
that what is not bound on earth cannot be bound in
heaven? If there is delay in binding on earth, will
there also be delay in heaven? Why must God wait for
the earth to bind before He binds that which He has
long desired to bind?

Let me say that by answering these questions a believer may become more useful in the hands of God.
We already know the reason for man's creation. God
creates man that the latter may be united with Him in
defeating Satan and his works. Being created with a
free will, man is expected to exercise his will for union
with God's will in opposing the will of Satan. This is
the purpose of creation as well as the purpose of
redemption. The entire life of the Lord Jesus demon-
strates this principle. Though we do not know the reason why, we nevertheless know that God will not act
independently. If the people of God fail to show sympathy towards Him by yielding their will to Him and
expressing their one mind with Him in prayer, He
would rather stand by and postpone his work. He refuses to act alone. He exalts His people by asking
them to work with Him. Although He is almighty, He
delights in having His almightiness circumscribed by

His children. However zealous He is towards His own will, He will temporarily permit Satan to be on the offensive should His people forget His will and fail to show sympathy by cooperating with Him.

Oh that God's children were not as cold as is evident today, that they were more willing to deny themselves and submit to God's will—caring more for His glory and keeping His word. Then would the eternal will of God concerning this age be speedily realized, the church would not be in such confusion, sinners would not be so hardened, the coming of the Lord Jesus and His kingdom would sooner arrive, Satan and his forces would be cast much earlier into the bottomless pit, and the knowledge of the Lord would more quickly spread over all the earth. Due to the fact that believers mind too much their own affairs and fail to work together with God, many enemies and much lawlessness are not bound, many sinners and much grace are not released. How greatly restricted is heaven by earth! Since God respects us so much, can we not trust Him that much?

How do we bind what God intends to bind? And loose what God intends to loose? The answer the Lord Jesus gives is this: "Agree on earth as touching anything that they shall ask." Now this is prayer—the prayer of the body of Christ. The peak of our working together with God is in asking with one accord that God will accomplish what He desires to accomplish. The true meaning of prayer is for the one who prays to pray for the fulfillment of the will of the One to whom he prays. Prayer is the occasion wherein to express our desire for God's will. Prayer means that our will is standing on God's side. Aside from this, there is no such thing as prayer.

Self and Prayer

How many prayers nowadays truly express the will of God? How much in our prayers is self completely forgotten and the will of the Lord is alone the thing that is sought? How many believers are really working together with God in prayer? How many of us are declaring daily before Him His will and pouring out our hearts in prayer that He may do whatever is His will that He has made known to us? Let it be clearly recognized that selfishness is no less evident in prayer than it is in other areas! How manifold are the askings for ourselves! How strong are our opinions, desires, plans and pursuits! Having so much of self, how can we expect to be able to forget ourselves completely and seek God's will in prayer? Self-denial must be practiced everywhere. It is just as essential in prayer as in action. We ought to know that we redeemed ones should live for the Lord—He who both died and now lives for us. We must live wholly for Him and seek nothing for ourselves. In our life of consecration, prayer is among the items to be consecrated.

A serious error concerning prayer prevails in our common understanding, which is to say, that we often think of prayer as an outlet for expressing what *we* need—as our cry to God for help. We do not see that prayer is the asking of God to fulfill *His* needs. We ought to understand that God's original thought is certainly not the letting of believers achieve their own aims through prayer, rather is it God accomplishing His purpose through the prayers of the believers. This is not meant to imply that Christians should never ask the Lord to supply their needs. It only is meant to indicate how we need first to understand the meaning and principles of prayer.

Whenever a believer is in want, he should first inquire: Will such lack affect God? Does He want me to be in need? Or is it His will to supply my need? When you see that God's will *is* to supply your need, you can then ask Him to fulfill His will by supplying what you need. Having come to know His will, you should now pray according to the will of God which you know. You pray that He will fulfill His will. The question is now no longer whether *your need* is met but whether *God's will* is done. Though your prayer today is not much different from that of the past, nonetheless what you now look for is that the Lord's will in this particular personal matter of yours may be done and not that your own need may be supplied. How many failures are registered right here: believers frequently assign to their own needs the priority; and even though they know that the Lord's will is to supply them, they nevertheless cannot forget to mention first in their prayers their own needs.

We should not just pray for our needs. In heaven and on earth there is only one prayer which is legitimate and acceptable to God—which is asking Him to fulfill His will. Our needs should be lost in God's will.

Whenever we see the will of God concerning our need, we should immediately lay down our need and ask Him to fulfill His will. To ask the Lord directly to supply our needs, whatever such needs may be, cannot be considered prayer of the highest level. Prayer for personal need should be touched indirectly by first asking the Lord's will to be done. This is the secret of prayer, the key to victory in prayer.

God's purpose is for us to be so filled with His will that we forget our own interests. He calls us to work together with Him for accomplishing His will. The way of working together is prayer. For this reason He wants us to learn in Him what His will is regarding all things so that we can then pray according to His will.

True prayer is a real work. Praying according to God's will and praying only for His will is indeed a self-denying work. Unless we are completely weaned from ourselves, having not the slightest interest of our own but living absolutely for the Lord and seeking only His glory, we will not like what He likes, nor seek what He seeks, nor pray what He wants us to pray. Without doubt, to work for God with no self-interest is very difficult; but to *pray* for Him without any self-interest is even harder. Even so, all who live for God must do this.

In past generations the Lord did not do many things which He is able and loves to do because of the lack of cooperation from His children. The failure lies not in God, but in His people. If we review our own personal histories we shall see the same sad state. Had we had greater faith and more prayer our life would not have been so ineffective. What the Lord now looks for is that His children may be willing to be united with His will and declare such union through prayer. No believer has ever fully experienced the greatness of accomplishment through union with God's will.

Prayer—Preparing the Way of God

A servant of the Lord has well said: Prayer is the rail for God's work. Indeed, prayer is to God's will as rails are to a train. The locomotive is full of power: it is capable of running a thousand miles a day. But if there are no rails, it cannot move forward a single inch. If it dares to move without them, it will soon sink into the earth. It may be able to travel over great distances, yet it cannot go to any place where no rails have been laid. And such is the relation between prayer and God's work. I do not believe it necessary to explain in detail, for I trust everyone can recognize the meaning of this parable. Without any doubt God is almighty and He works mightily, but He will not and cannot work if you and I do not labor together with Him in prayer, prepare the way for His will, and pray "with all prayer and supplication" (Eph. 6.18) to grant Him the maneuverability to so work. Many are the things which God wills to do and would like to do, but His hands are bound because His children do not sympathize with Him and have not prayed so as to prepare ways for Him. Let me say to all who have wholly given themselves to God: Do examine yourselves and see if in this respect you have limited Him day after day.

Hence our most important work is to prepare the way of the Lord. There is no other work which can be compared with this work. With God there are many "possibilities"; but these will turn into "impossibilities" if believers do not open up ways for Him. In view of this, our prayers in one mind with God must be greatly increased. May we pray exhaustively—that is to say, may we pray through in all directions—so that God's will may prosper at all points. Though our activities among men are important, our working together with the Lord by prayers offered up before Him is much more important.

Prayer is not an attempt to restore heaven's heart. It is a most erroneous concept to hold that God being hard, we therefore need to engage in combat against Him in prayer so as to subjugate Him and thereby cause Him to alter His decision. Whatever prayer is not according to God's will is utterly void. Let us see that we strive before God as if in conflict only because His will is being blocked by either men or the devil, and so, we greatly desire Him to execute His will in order that His own determinate will may not suffer because of opposition. By so desiring after God's determinate will and praying—yea, even striving—against all that oppose His will, we prepare the way for Him to carry out His determinate will without permitting that which comes out of man or of the devil temporarily to prevail. True, we seem to be striving against God; yet such striving is not aimed against God as though to compel Him to change His will to suit our pleasure, but in reality is against all that is opposed to God so that He may fulfill His will. In view of this, let us see that we are unable to pray as fellow-workers of God unless we really know what His will is.

Having now understood somewhat the true meaning of prayer, let us be doubly careful lest the flesh slip in. For please note that if God by himself sends out laborers, then Christ would not have ordered us to pray to the Lord of the harvest that He send forth laborers! If God's name will quite naturally be hallowed, if His kingdom is to come without any need for our cooperation, and if His will shall be done automatically on earth, the Lord Jesus would never have taught us to pray in such a manner as He did. If He himself shall return without the need of a response from His church, the Spirit of the Lord would not have moved the apostle John to cry out for His quick coming back. If God the Father will just spontaneously make the believers one, would our Lord have ever prayed to His Father to this effect? If working together with God is not essential, what can possibly be the use of the continuous intercession of our Lord in heaven?

Oh let us see that prayer in sympathy with God is more vital than any other thing! For God can only work in matters for which His children have shown sympathy. He refuses to work in areas where there are no prayers and where His people's will is not united with His will. Prayer with joined wills is real prayer. The highest motive of prayer is not in having it answered. It is to join man's will with God's so that He may be able to work. Sometimes we may ask incorrectly and thus our prayer goes unanswered; yet if our will is joined with God's, He will still gain, for through our sympathy He is still able to work out His will.

2 | Pray According to God's Will

And this is the boldness which we have toward him, that, if we ask anything according to His will, he hears us. (1 John 5.14)

I anticipated the dawning of the morning, and cried: I hoped in thy words. Mine eyes anticipated the night-watches, that I might meditate on thy word. (Ps. 119.147, 148)

In the third year of Cyrus King of Persia, a thing was revealed unto Daniel, whose name was called Belteshazzar; and the thing was true, even a great warfare: and he understood the thing, and had understanding of the vision. In those days I, Daniel, was mourning three whole weeks. I ate no pleasant bread, neither came flesh nor wine into my mouth, neither did I anoint myself at all, till three whole weeks were fulfilled ... Then said he unto me, Fear not, Daniel; for from the first day that thou didst set thy heart to understand, and to humble thyself before thy God, thy words were heard: and I am come for thy words' sake. But the prince of the kingdom

of Persia withstood me one and twenty days ... Then
said he, Knowest thou wherefore I am come unto thee?
and now will I return to fight with the prince of Persia:
and when I go forth, lo, the prince of Greece shall come.
But I will tell thee that which is inscribed in the writing
of truth ... (Dan. 10.1–21)

As we read Daniel chapter 10 which tells us of
how Daniel prayed, we should notice at least two
points.

Point One

The first point to be noticed is that one who really
prays is a person who not only often approaches God
but also whose will frequently enters into God's will—
that is to say, his thought often enters into God's
thought. This is a most important principle in prayer.

There is a kind of prayer which originates entirely
from our need. Though at times the Lord hears such
prayers, He nonetheless gets little or nothing out of
them. Please take note of this verse: "He gave them
their request, but sent leaness into their soul" (Ps.
106.15). What does this passage mean? As Israel
cried to God for the gratification of their lust, He did
answer them by indeed giving them what they asked
for—but with the result, however, of their being weak-
ened before Him. Oh yes, sometimes God will hear
and respond to your prayers for the sake of satisfying
your own needs, yet His own will is not fulfilled. Let

us see that such prayer does not have much value in it.

But there is another kind of prayer, which comes out of God's own need. It is of God, and it is initiated by God. And such prayer is most valuable. In order to have such prayer, the one who prays must not only personally often appear before God but also he must allow his will to enter into God's will, his thought must be allowed to enter into God's thought. Since he habitually lives in the Lord's presence, such a person is given to know His will and thoughts. And these divine wills and thoughts quite naturally become his own desires, which he then expresses in prayer.

Oh how we must learn this second kind of prayer. Although we are immature and weak, we may nevertheless approach God and let His Spirit bring our will into God's will and our thought into God's thought. As we touch a little of His will and thought we come to understand a little more of how He works and what He requires of us. So that gradually the will and thought of God which we have known and entered into becomes in us our prayer. And such prayer is of great value.

Having entered into God's thought and thus having touched His will and purpose, Daniel found in his own heart the same desire as God's. The longing of God was reproduced in Daniel and became Daniel's desire. So that when he expressed this desire in prayer with cries and groanings, he was actually articulating God's desire. We need to have this kind of prayer, for it really touches the divine heart. We do not need more words; what we need is a touching more of the

Lord's mind. Let the Spirit of God lead us into the intent of God's heart.

Of course, this kind of prayer will require time to learn. In the beginning of such a learning process let us not seek for more words nor for more thoughts. Our spirit should be calm and restful. We may bring our current situation to the Lord and consider it in the light of His countenance, or we may forget our present condition and simply meditate on His word before Him. Or we may just live before Him and try to touch Him with our spirit. As a matter of fact, it is not we who go forth to meet God but it is God who is waiting there for us. And there in His presence we perceive something and touch upon the will of God. The greatest wisdom comes, in fact, from this very source. By this, our will enters into His will and our thought enters into His heart. And from there our prayer will rise to Him.

As we bring our will and thought to God His own will and thought begin to be reproduced in us, and then this becomes our will and thought. This kind of prayer is most valuable and full of weight. Let us recall what the Lord Jesus said about prayer: "After this manner therefore pray ye: Our Father who art in heaven, hallowed by thy name. Thy kingdom come. Thy will be done, as in heaven, so on earth" (Matt. 6.9,10). These are not just three words for us to repeat. These words, which disclose the will and thought of God, are to be reproduced in us when the Spirit of God brings our mind to God. And as they become our will and thought, the prayer which we afterwards utter is most valuable and most weighty.

Over the one and the same matter there is the possibility of having two different kinds of prayer. One kind has its source in our own will. It is based on our own thinking and our own expectations. The Lord may hear and answer our prayer, but such prayer has a very low value attached to it. If, on the other hand, we bring this matter before God and let His Spirit merge our will into God's will and our thought into God's thought, we shall discover within us a deep longing which is in fact a reproduction of His will and thought. Suppose the Lord is grieved and mournful over the death of men. We too will develop such a burden of not willing to see even one soul perish. And such is a reproduction of God's heart which enables us to pray with inward sighings. Or if the Lord is anxious and hurt because of the failure of His children, this very same burden will be reproduced in us; with the result that we will have the same yearning of not willing to see a child of God fall into sin and darkness. Then prayer and intercession will issue forth from within us. There we will confess, plead for forgiveness, and ask God to purify His children.

Hence one kind of prayer is prayed according to our own will; the other kind is prayed as the will of God which has been reproduced in us and has become our will. How different are these two kinds of prayer. In the latter case, as any believer approaches God, the will of God will be reproduced in him. It will become his breath and his sigh. And prayer which is prayed according to this will has worth and weight.

God has many things to do on earth, touching many areas. How, then, can we ever pray according to our own feeling and thought? We should draw near to God and allow Him to impress us with what He desires to do so that we ourselves may intercede with groanings. In case, as we approach Him, God puts His will of spreading the gospel in us, this soon will become a burden in us. And when we pray according to that burden, we shall have a sense as though our very sigh is divulging the will of God. The Lord may put a variety of wills or reproduce a variety of burdens in us. But whatever be the particular will or burden, whenever it is reproduced in a person's heart, that person is able to make the Lord's will his own will and pray it out accordingly. When, in the case of Daniel, he came before God, he touched a certain matter; and then we saw that he prayed out that thing with deep groanings. How precious and substantial is prayer such as this. It can hallow God's name, bring in God's kingdom, and cause God's will to prevail on earth as in heaven.

Point Two

The second point to be noticed is, that when we pray with such prayer, our prayer will shake up hell and affect Satan. For this reason, Satan will rise up to hinder such prayer. All prayers which come from God touch the powers of darkness. Here involves spiritual warfare. Perhaps our physical bodies, our families, or whatever pertains to us will be attacked by Satan. For whenever there is such prayer, it calls forth Satanic assault. The enemy so attacks in order that our prayer might be discontinued. He may even try to throw up some blockage in the air so as to delay the answer to prayer. That prayer ought to receive a response quickly; however, the answer seems to be suspended in the air. In just such fashion as this, the answer to Daniel's prayer was hindered for twenty-one days although God actually heard him the day he began to pray. In such a situation, what did Daniel do? He knelt before God and he waited until the answer to prayer arrived.

Let me ask this question: Do you ever wonder why your prayer remains unanswered? Perhaps it is suspended somewhere, still within the period of twenty-one days! The answer of the throne may possibly have been given, yet it encounters opposition and, consequently, is suspended in air. Why? It awaits more prayers on earth; it needs people who will patiently and humbly wait upon God.

Oh do draw near to God's presence, calm down before Him, lay aside your own thoughts, and enter into His thought. You will then realize the significance of prayer and see in how many matters God is waiting for you to pray. Things around the entire world are to be subjects of your prayer, and matters in all directions are to be touched through your prayer. You do not pray according to your own feeling; you instead bring your own heart desire to the heart desire of God and let His will become your will, your groaning, and your hope in the universe.

Nothing of the will of God is ever released without passing through man, and nothing of whatever will of God released through man is ever free from an encounter with the power of Satan. For the realization of God's will, there is the need for prayer; to remove Satan's opposition requires prayer. Let us exercise the authority of prayer in loosing whatever must be loosed and binding whatever should be bound. Let us not pray after our own will. Let us draw near to God and pray according to the will which He has reproduced in us. When God says that this must be done we also say it must be done. When He says this must not exist, we too say it must not exist. We ought to forget ourselves, touch God's will, and express His current will through prayer.

3 | Prayer and God's Work

With all prayer and supplication praying at all seasons in the Spirit, and watching thereunto in all perseverance and supplication. (Eph. 6.18)

Thus saith the Lord Jehovah: For this, moreover, will I be inquired of by the house of Israel, to do it for them: I will increase them with men like a flock. (Ezek. 36.37)

I have set watchmen upon thy walls, O Jerusalem; they shall never hold their peace day or night: ye that are Jehovah's remembrancers, take ye no rest, and give him no rest, till he establish, and till he make Jerusalem a praise in the earth. (Is. 62.6, 7)

One

When God works, He does so with specific law and definite principle. Even though He could do whatever pleases Him, yet he never acts carelessly. He always performs according to His determinate law and principle. Unquestionably He can transcend all these laws and principles, for He is God and is quite capable of acting according to His own pleasure. Nonetheless, we discover a most marvelous fact in the Bible; which is, that in spite of His exceeding greatness and His ability to operate according to His will, God ever acts along the line of the law or principle which He has laid down. It seems as though He deliberately puts himself under the law to be controlled by His own law.

Now then, what is the principle of God's working? God's working has a primal principle behind it, which is, that He wants man to pray, that He desires man to cooperate with Him through prayer.

There was once a Christian who well knew how to pray. He declared this, that all spiritual works include four steps: The first step is that God conceives a thought, which is His will: The second step is that God reveals this will to His children through the Holy Spirit, causing them to know that He has a will, a plan, a demand and expectation: The third step is that God's children return His will by praying to Him, for prayer is responding to God's will—if our heart is wholly one with His heart, we will naturally voice in our prayer what He intends to do: And the fourth step is that God will accomplish this very thing.

Here we are concerned not with the first step nor with the second, but with the third step—how we are to return God's will by praying to Him. Please notice the word "return". All prayers with worth possess this element of return in them. If our prayer is only for the purpose of accomplishing our plan and expectations it does not have much value in the spiritual realm. Prayer must originate from God and be responded to by us. Such alone is meaningful prayer, since God's *work* is controlled by such prayer. How many things the Lord indeed desires to do, yet He does not perform them because His people do not pray. He will wait until men agree with Him, and then He will work. This is a great principle in God's working, and it constitutes one of the most important principles to be found in the Bible.

Two

The word in Ezekiel 36.37 is quite surprising. The Lord says He has a purpose, which is, that He will increase the house of Israel with men like a flock. This is the determinate will of God. What He ordains He will perform. Nevertheless, He will not accomplish it instantly but will wait awhile. What is the reason for the waiting? The Lord says, "For this, moreover, will I be inquired of by the house of Israel, to do it for them." He has decided to increase the house of Israel with men, but He must wait till the children of Israel inquire of Him about the matter. Let us see that even if He himself has resolved to perform certain things He will not do so immediately. He will wait until men show their agreement before He proceeds. Each time He works He never goes ahead immediately simply because He has His will; no, He will wait, if necessary, for His people to express their agreement in prayer before He does act. This assuredly is a most amazing phenomenon.

Let us always be mindful of this truth, that all spiritual works are decided by God and desired by His children—all are initiated by God and approved by His children. This is a great principle in spiritual work. "For this, moreover, will I be inquired of by the house of Israel," says the Lord. His work awaits the inquiring of the children of Israel. And one day the Israelites really inquired, and without delay He performed it for them.

Do we see this principle of God's work? After He has initiated something, He pauses in its execution until we pray. Since the time of the founding of the church, there is nothing God does on earth without the prayer of His children. From the moment He has His children, He does everything according to the prayer of His own. He puts everything in their prayer. We do not know why He acts in such a way; but we do know that this is a fact. God is willing to condescend himself to such a position of taking delight in fulfilling His will through His children.

There is another illustration of this in Isaiah 62: "I have set watchmen upon thy walls, O Jerusalem; they shall never hold their peace day or night: ye that are Jehovah's remembrancers, take ye no rest, and give him no rest, till he establish, and till he make Jerusalem a praise in the earth" (v.6,7). God intends to make Jerusalem a praise in the earth. How does He realize it? He sets watchmen upon its walls that they may cry to Him. How should they cry? "Take ye no rest, and give him no rest"—we are to cry to Him unceasingly and give Him no rest. We keep on praying until He accomplishes His work. Although the Lord has already willed to make Jerusalem a praise in the earth, He nonetheless sets watchmen on its walls. By their prayer will He perform. He urges them not to pray just once, but to pray without ceasing. Keep on praying till His will is done. In other words, the will of God is governed by the prayers of man. The Lord waits for us to pray. Let us understand clearly that as regards the *content* of God's will it is entirely decided by God himself; we do not make, nor even participate in, the decision. Yet concerning the *doing* of His will it is governed by our prayer.

A brother once observed that God's will is like a train whereas our prayer is like the rails of a train. A train may travel to any place, except that it must run on rails. It has tremendous power to go east, west, south and north, but it can only run to places where rails have been laid. So that it is not because God has no power (He, like a train, *has* power, great power); but because He chooses to be governed by man's prayer, therefore all valuable prayers (like a train's rails) pave the way for God. Consequently, if we do not take up the responsibility of prayer, we will hinder the fulfillment of God's will.

Three

When God created man He gave him a free will. There thus exist in the universe three different wills; namely, the will of God, the will of Satan the enemy, and the will of man. People may wonder why the Lord does not destroy Satan in a moment's time. The Lord could, but He has not done so. And why? Because He wants man to cooperate with Him in dealing with Satan. Now God has His will, Satan has his, and man has his too. God seeks to have man's will joined with His. He will not destroy Satan all by himself. We do not know entirely why God has chosen this way, but we do know He delights in doing it this way—namely, that He will not act independently; He looks for the cooperation of man. And this is the responsibility of the church on earth.

When the Lord wishes to do a thing He first puts His own thought in us through the Holy Spirit. Only after we have turned this thought into prayer will He perform it. Such is the procedure of divine working; God will not work out anything in any other way. He needs the cooperation of us men. He needs a will that is one with His will and is sympathetic to Him. If God does everything without involving us men, then there is absolutely no need for us to be here on earth, nor do we need to know what His will is. Yet every will of God must be done by us, since He calls for our will to be one with His own.

Thus the first step in our doing God's will is for us to utter His will in prayer. God's will is uttered through our prayer. Here may we see that prayer is indeed a work. There is no work more important than prayer because the latter accomplishes as well as expresses the will of God. Hence all prayer which comes out of self-will is useless. Prayers which are in accordance with God's will originate from God, are revealed to us by the Holy Spirit, and return to God through prayers. Whatever prayer is in accordance with God's will must begin with God's will; men merely respond to, and transmit, this will. All which commence with us are prayers of no spiritual worth.

As we read through church history, we may notice that every great revival has always come from prayer. This shows us how prayer enables the Lord to do what He desires to do. We cannot ask Him to do what He does not want to do, though we may certainly *delay* what He wishes to do. God is absolute; therefore, we cannot change Him, neither can we force Him to do what He does not want to do, nor can we persuade Him *not* to do what He wants to do. Even so, when we are called to be the channel of His will we may doubtless block God's work if we do not cooperate with Him.

For this reason, our prayer should never be asking the Lord to do what He has no desire to do or trying to change His will. It is simply a praying out of His will, thus enabling Him to do what He desires to do. In case we beg strongly with the expectation of forcing Him to do that which He has no intention of doing, we are wasting our effort, for our prayer is of no avail. If God is not willing to act, who can make Him act? One thing only can we do, and that is, we can pray out what God has desired. Then will He accomplish His work because we are one with Him.

Take, as an example, the coming of the Holy Spirit on the day of Pentecost. Hundreds of years before the day of Pentecost, even at the time of Joel,

God had already mentioned this coming. But the Holy Spirit came down only after many disciples had gathered and prayed. Although the advent of the Spirit had long before been determined by God, it did not come to pass until people had prayed. The Lord is capable of doing many things; yet He likes to do them after men have prayed. He is waiting for our consent. He himself is already willing, but He wants us to be willing too. How many are the things He has decided to do, and yet He waits, because we have not expressed to Him our agreement. May we see that although we cannot force God to do what He does not want to do, we nevertheless can certainly ask Him to do what He undoubtedly wants to do. Frequently we miss spiritual blessing because we fail to express God's will in prayer.

If anyone will rise up and devote himself to the work of prayer exclusively, how excellent that will be. God is waiting for such ones to work together with Him so as to enable Him to finish His work. Some Christians may ask why the Lord does not save more sinners, why He does not cause every believer to overcome. I sincerely believe that He would undoubtedly do such works if people would only pray. He is not unwilling to work, He simply wants first to obtain a people who will work together with Him. Whenever people begin working with Him, He performs immediately. In all spiritual works, the Lord is always waiting for an expression of desire from His children. Whether or not a matter is done is dependent upon how His children pray. We therefore ought to declare our cooperation with Him. God is waiting to bless us. The question now is: Will we pray?

Those who do not know God may retort on this wise: If God wants to do something, why does He not just do it, why should He desire men to pray? Is He not all knowing? Will God not be annoyed by much prayer? Let us keep in mind, however, that we humans are free-will beings. As the Lord cannot deny His own will, so He will not coerce ours. He will wait for us if His will is not prayed forth by us. Yet does He not want His will to be done on earth as it is in heaven? Why then does He not go ahead and perform it? Why does the Lord ask His disciples to pray: "Our Father who art in heaven, ... thy will be done, as in heaven, so on earth"? If He wants His kingdom to come, why does it not come automatically? Why must the disciples pray, "Thy kingdom come"? Why, if God doubtless desires His name to be hallowed by all men, does He not make it so by himself instead of His requiring the disciples to pray: "Hallowed be thy name"? All this is for no other reason than the fact that God himself does not wish to do anything independently, because He chooses to have men cooperate with Him. He has the power, but He needs our prayers to lay the tracks down for the train of His will to run on. The more tracks we lay, the more abundant will be the works of God. Our prayers should therefore serve the purpose of laying down a huge spiritual network of railroad tracks. And the more the better.

Four

How should we lay tracks for the will of God? The answer: "With all prayer and supplication praying at all seasons in the Spirit" (Eph. 6.18). Our prayer should touch in many directions. We should pray constantly. Pray specific prayers as well as general ones. Many of our prayers are too thinly spread; there are too many holes by which Satan is given plenty of opportunities to slip in. Were our prayers well-rounded and tightly guarded, he would have no chance to do havoc.

When, for example, a brother goes out to preach you should lay rails for him so that God's will might be fulfilled in him. If you pray only a few words of general prayer, asking the Lord to bless him, protect him, and supply his needs, such a prayer net is too thinly spread. If you want to pray for a particular person you should spread for him a very tight net so that Satan can find no hole through which to creep in. How, then, ought you to pray? As the brother in question is preparing to leave, you should pray for his health, his luggage, the train he will ride, even the time of the train, his rest and food on the train, and people he will meet on the train. You should also pray for everything he will be involved in after he disembarks: pray for the place where he will stay, pray for the neighbors, even pray for the things he will read, also pray for his work—the time involved in it as well as all other things connected with the work. If you pray for him as extensively as this, it will be most difficult for Satan to find a loophole through which to attack him. The work of prayer is therefore a real work. All who are lazy, foolish, and careless cannot do such work. Yet how often, when there are those who earnestly and extensively pray for a certain thing, the thing is found to be done.

There is another lesson we should learn here. Satan is so full of wiles that it is really hard for us to outguess him. We are unable to pray over every last detail, and hence we can only pray in this manner: "O Lord, may Your precious blood answer whatever comes from Satan." Let us realize that the precious blood of Christ is the answer to all the works of the enemy. Such prayer is the best one that can be offered against him, so that he can never get through this net to assault God's people.

Each time we pray, we need to see three aspects: first, we must see to whom we are praying; second, we must know for whom we pray; and third, we ought to realize against whom we are praying. Frequently we only remember two aspects of prayer—those concerning God (to whom we pray) and men (for whom we pray). And thus we have overlooked the enemy aspect. In this matter of prayer we should know not only *to* whom we pray but also *against* whom we pray. We should know *for* whom we pray but we should also know that there is an enemy who lurks around to hurt us. Our prayer is directed towards God, for men, and against Satan. If we take care of these three aspects, God will surely work for us.

Everyone who truly works for the Lord must

spread the net of prayer so that He may work through that person. God is not at all unwilling to work: He is simply waiting for people to pray. How He waits expectantly for men to have a prayer life, how His will awaits the prayers of men. Oftentimes, without your setting a time for prayer beforehand, you sense a burden to pray. This indicates that there is one item in God's will which requires your prayer. Pray when you feel the burden of prayer—this is praying according to God's will. It is the Holy Spirit who constrains you to pray out the prayer which is in accordance with the will of God. When the Holy Spirit is urging you to pray, you should do so. If you do not pray, you will feel suffocated within as if there is something left undone. In the event you still do not pray, you will feel even more weighed down. Finally, if you do not pray at all, the spirit of prayer as well as the burden of prayer will be so dulled that it will be difficult for you to regain such feeling and to pray the prayer according to God's will afterwards.

Each time God puts a prayer thought into us His Holy Spirit first moves us into having a burden to pray for that particular matter. As soon as we receive such feeling we should immediately give ourselves to prayer. We should pay the cost of praying well for this matter. For when we are moved by the Holy Spirit our own spirit instantly senses a burden as though something were being laid upon our heart. After we pray it out we feel relieved as though having a heavy stone removed from off us. But in case we do not pour it out in prayer, we will get the feeling of something not yet done. If we do not pray it out we are not in harmony with God's heart. Were we to be faithful in prayer, that is to say, were we to pray as soon as the burden comes upon us, prayer would not become a weight, it would instead be light and pleasant.

What a pity that so many people quench the Holy Spirit here. They quench the sensation which the Holy Spirit gives to move them to pray. Hereafter, few of such sensations will ever come upon them. Thus they are no longer useful vessels before the Lord. The Lord can achieve nothing through them since they are no longer able to breathe out in prayer the will of God. Oh, if ever we fall to such an extent of having no prayer burden, we will have sunk indeed into a most perilous situation, for we have already lost communion with God and He is no more able to use us in His work. For this reason, we must be extra careful in dealing with the feeling which the Holy Spirit gives to us. Whenever there is a prayer burden we should immediately inquire of the Lord, saying, "O God, what do you want me to pray for? What is it which you wish to accomplish that needs me to pray?" And were we to pray it out, we would be entrusted by God with the next prayer. If our first burden is not yet discharged, we are unable to take up the second load.

Let us ask the Lord to make us faithful prayer partners. As soon as the burden comes, we have it discharged by praying it out. If the burden grows too heavy and it cannot be discharged by prayer, then we should fast. When prayer cannot discharge a burden, fasting must follow. Through fasting, the burden of prayer may quickly be discharged, since fasting is able to help us discharge the heaviest of burdens.

If anyone should continue on in performing the work of prayer, he will become a channel for the will of God. Whenever the Lord has anything to do, He will seek that person out. Let me say this, that the will of God is always in search of a way out. The Lord is always apprehending someone or some people to be the expression of His will. If many will rise up to do this work, He will do many things because of their prayers.

4 | The Principle of Praying Thrice

And he left them again, and went away, and prayed a
third time, saying again the same words. (Matt. 26.44)

Concerning this thing I besought the Lord thrice,
that it might depart from me. (2 Cor. 12.8)

There is one particular secret about prayer that we
should know about, which is, a praying three times to
the Lord. This "thrice" is not limited to only three
times, it may be many times. The Lord Jesus asked
God three times in the garden of Gethsemane until
His prayer was heard—at which point He stopped.
Paul too prayed to God three times, and ceased praying after he was given God's word. Hence all prayers
should heed the principle of thrice. This "thrice" does
not mean that we need only pray once, twice, and
three times, and then stop. It simply signifies the fact
that before we stop we must pray thoroughly until
God hears us.

This principle of three times is most significant. Not only in our personal prayer do we need to pay attention to such a principle, even in our prayer meetings we must attend to it. If we expect our prayer in a prayer meeting to fulfill the ministry of the church in accomplishing whatever God wants us to accomplish, we should well remember this important principle.

The principle of praying thrice is to pray thoroughly, a praying through until we are clear on God's will, until we obtain His answer. In a prayer meeting, never reflect that since a matter has already been prayed for by a certain brother it does not need my prayer anymore. For example, a sister is sick and we pray for her. Not because one brother has already prayed for that sister do I not need to add my prayer. No, that brother has prayed once, I may pray the second time, and another may pray the third time. This does not imply that each prayer must be prayed by three persons. Prayer must be offered with burden. Sometimes we may have to pray five or ten times. What is important is that there needs to be prayer till the burden is discharged. This is the principle of praying thrice. This is the secret to success in a prayer meeting.

Let us not allow our prayer to jump about like a grasshopper: hopping to another matter before the first one is thoroughly prayed through, and before this second matter is thoroughly prayed for, we are found skipping back to the very first matter. Such hopping-around prayer does not discharge burdens, and is therefore difficult to obtain God's answer. Such prayer has little use and does not fulfill the ministry of prayer.

In order to fulfill the ministry of prayer we must have a burden for prayer before God. We do not intend to set up a law; we only wish to present this principle here. Let us recognize this one thing: burden is the secret of prayer. If a person does not feel within him burden to pray for a particular matter he can hardly succeed in prayer. In a prayer meeting some brothers and sisters may mention a great many subjects for prayer. But if you are not touched inwardly, you cannot pray. Therefore every brother and sister who comes to a prayer meeting ought to have prayer burden so as to pray.

At the same time do not be totally absorbed in only considering what burden you yourself have; you should also sense the burdens of other brothers and sisters in the meeting. For example, one sister may be troubled by her husband; one brother may be sick. If in a prayer meeting one person asks God to save the sister's husband, and this is followed by another person who asks God to heal the brother's sickness, and in turn this is followed by still another individual who remembers before God something else, then each person is only praying for his own particular matter. Such prayer is not in accordance with the principle of praying thrice. For in the example just given, what is happening is that before one matter has been thoroughly prayed for the second topic is already being prayed for. Consequently, in a prayer meeting the brethren who are gathered must notice if a prayer burden for the first matter has been discharged. If all pray for that sister and the prayer burden is discharged, the believers can then pray for the sick brother. Before the prayer burden of the first topic has been lifted, those praying together should not switch to the second and third subjects of prayer. Suppose the entire gathering is yet involved with one particular matter. Then no one present should try to inject another prayer that is only according to his own personal feeling.

Brethren should learn to touch the spirit of the entire gathering. They must learn to enter into the feeling of the whole assembly. Let us see that some matters may only need to be prayed once and the burden for such is over and done with. But other matters perhaps need to be prayed twice. While still other matters probably have to be prayed three or five times before the various burdens for them are discharged. Irrespective of the number of times, the burden must be discharged before prayer on a particular item is ended. The principle of praying three times is none other than to pray until the burden is lifted.

In all this, of course, believers should also understand the difference between personal prayer and corporate prayer. When one is praying alone he thinks only of his personal burdens; but in corporate prayer each one should notice the burden of the meeting instead of paying attention to one's own burdens alone. Hence in a prayer meeting the brethren must learn to sense the feeling of the gathering. For some items, praying once for each of them is enough. There is no need to pray again, since the assembly has no longer any burden for it. But for other items, praying once is not sufficient. Each of these matters needs to be prayed for again and possibly a third or fifth time. Before one burden is discharged, no one should commence to pray about another item. All must wait until the first burden has been lifted and then someone can change to another subject as the Lord gives another burden for prayer.

So in the prayer meeting, let us learn to pray over a matter by allowing one person, two persons, three or five persons to pray as necessary. Yet not in the sense of each praying his own prayer, but a praying with one accord as we gather together. Praying with one accord is something we must learn. A person may be able to pray by his own self, five persons may all be capable of praying respectively, but all of us, when we come together must learn a new way of praying, which is a praying with one accord. Let us see that corporate prayer does not come automatically; it has to be learned.

"If two of you shall agree on earth as touching anything that they shall ask, it shall be done for them of my Father who is in heaven" (Matt.18.19). This is not a small concern. We should learn how to sense the feeling of others, learn to touch what is called the prayer of the church, and learn when a prayer burden has been lifted. And thus will we know how to fulfill in the meeting the ministry of prayer.

5 | Prayer That Resists Satan

And he spake a parable unto them to the end that they ought always to pray, and not to faint; saying, There was in a city a judge, who feared not God, and regarded not man: and there was a widow in that city; and she came oft unto him, saying, Avenge me of mine adversary. And he would not for a while: but afterward he said within himself, Though I fear not God, nor regard man; yet because this widow troubleth me, I will avenge her, lest she wear me out by her continual coming. And the Lord said, Hear what the unrighteous judge saith. And shall not God avenge his elect, that cry to him day and night, and yet he is long-suffering over them? I say unto you, that he will avenge them speedily. Nevertheless, when the Son of man cometh, shall he find faith on the earth? (Luke 18.1–8)

The Three Aspects of Prayer

Our prayer has these three aspects: (1) we our-

selves, (2) the God to whom we pray, and (3) our
enemy, Satan. Every true prayer is related to all three
aspects. When we come to pray, we naturally pray for
our own welfare. We have needs, wants and expectations; and so we pray. We pray for the sake of fulfilling our requests. Even so, in true prayer we should
not simply ask concerning those things pertaining to
our own welfare, we should also pray for the glory of
God and for heaven's rule over the earth. Although in
having prayer answered we who pray are benefited as
the immediate beneficiaries, the reality in the spiritual
realm shows likewise that the Lord gets glory and that
His will is done. Answer to prayer gives the Lord
much glory, for it reveals the exceeding greatness of
His love and power in fulfilling the request of His
children. It also indicates that His will is done, because He will not answer prayer which is not in accordance with His will.

The petitioners are we; the petitioned is God. In a
successful prayer, both the petitioner and the petitioned gain. The petitioner obtains his heart desire,
and the petitioned gets His will done. This we do not
need to dwell on at any length, since all of the Lord's
faithful children who have some experience in prayer
know the relation between those two aspects in prayer.
But what we would like to remind believers of now is
the fact that if in prayer we only attend to these two
aspects of God and man, our prayer is yet imperfect.
Even though it may be quite effective, there nevertheless is defeat in success for we still have not mastered
the true meaning of prayer. No doubt all spiritual be-

lievers are aware of the absolute relationship between prayer and God's glory and will. Prayer is not just for our own profit. Still, such knowledge is incomplete— we must also notice the third aspect: that as we pray to the Lord, what we ask and what God promises will unquestionably hurt His enemy.

We know the ruler of this universe is God. Yet Satan is called "the prince of the world" (John 14.30) since "the whole world lieth in the evil one" (1 John 5.19). Hence we see that there are two diametrically opposing forces in this world, each seeking for ascendancy. God in truth has the ultimate victory; nonetheless, in this age of ours before the millennial kingdom, Satan continues to usurp power in this world to oppose God's work, will, and interest. We who are children of God belong to God. If we gain anything under His hand, it naturally will mean that His enemy suffers loss. The amount of gain we make is the amount of God's will done. And the amount of God's will done is in turn the amount of loss Satan suffers.

Since we belong to God, Satan intends to frustrate, afflict, or suppress us and allow us no foothold. This is his aim, although his aim may not be achieved because we may approach the throne of grace by the precious blood of the Lord Jesus, asking for God's protection and care. As God hears our prayer, Satan's plan is definitely defeated. In answering our prayer God thwarts the evil will of Satan, and consequently the latter is not able to ill-treat us according to this scheme. Whatever we gain in prayer is the enemy's loss. So that our gain and the Lord's glory are in inverse proportion to Satan's loss. One gains, the other loses; one loses and the other gains. In view of this, we in our prayer should not only consider our own welfare and the glory and will of God but also observe the third aspect—that which pertains to the enemy, Satan. A prayer that does not take into consideration all three aspects is superficial, of little worth, and without much accomplishment.

We have no need to talk about those prayers which are superficial, nonsensical and heartless—for they have no effect upon any of the three aspects of prayer. In the case of a carnal Christian, even his sensible prayer lays stress solely on the one aspect of his own welfare. His motive in prayer is to benefit himself. What he has in mind is merely his own needs and wants. If only he can have the Lord answer his prayer and give him his heart desire, then he is satisfied. He does not recognize that there is such a thing as the will of God, nor is he aware of what the glory of God is. And of course he does not have the remotest concept concerning the aspect of making Satan suffer loss.

But not all believers are carnal. We thank and praise the Lord for the many among His children who are spiritual. When they pray, their purpose is not so selfish as to be satisfied if the Lord will only answer their prayer in supplying their personal needs. They also pay great attention to the glory and will of God. They expect Him to answer their prayer not because they only want to get something for themselves but because additionally He will be glorified in the answer to their prayer. In praying, they do not insist on hav-

ing what they pray for, because they care for the will
of God alone. Concerning that will, it is not a matter
of whether the Lord is pleased to grant their petition
but whether such answer to prayer shall conflict or not
with the will of God's work, government and plan. Attention is paid not only to the matter for prayer itself
but also to the relation of such a prayer matter to the
broad perspective of the Lord's work. Hence their
prayer covers the two aspects of both God and man.

Nevertheless, very few Christians consider the
third aspect—that of Satan—in their prayer. The aim
of a true prayer touches on not just personal gain
(sometimes this aspect is not even thought of) but
more importantly on the glory of God and the loss of
the enemy. They do not reckon their own welfare to be
of prime importance. They instead consider their
prayer to be highly successful if it will cause Satan to
lose and God to be glorified. What they look for in
their prayer is the enemy's loss. Their view is not
restricted to their immediate environment but they
take as their perspective God's work and will in the
whole world. Yet let me add that this is not to suggest
that they only take into account the aspects of God
and Satan and entirely forget the personal aspect of
prayer. As a matter of fact, when God's will is done
and Satan suffers loss they will unquestionably be
profited themselves. The spiritual progress of a saint
can therefore be judged by the emphasis to be seen in
his prayer.

The Parable of Luke 18

In the parable recorded in Luke 18.1–8 our Lord
Jesus touches upon all three features in prayer of
which we have been speaking. In this connection,
please note that we find three persons mentioned in
the parable, namely: (1) the judge, (2) the widow, and
(3) the adversary. The judge (in a negative way)
represents God, the widow is representative of the
church today or individual faithful Christians, while
the adversary stands for our enemy the devil. When
we explain this parable we frequently pay attention
only to the relation between the judge and the widow.
We note how this judge, who neither fears God nor regards men, finally avenges the widow because of her
incessant coming; and, we conclude, since our God is
not at all virtueless as is this judge, will He not surely
avenge us speedily if we pray? Now this is about all
that we explain from this parable.

Yet too many of us are unaware of the fact that we
are neglecting another important person in the parable. Let us see that if there is no adversary, would this
widow find it necessary to go to the judge? Yet she is
driven to seek out the judge because she is oppressed
by the adversary. Especially when we consider the
words which this widow says to the judge, we cannot
fail to recognize the place the adversary has in the
story. For the sake of brevity the Scripture merely records these few words: "Avenge me of mine adversary"—yet how very much is contained in such a short
sentence! Does it not tell of a most agonizing situa-

tion? Asking for vengeance reveals that there are wrongs. Where do such wrongs and grievances come from? None other than from the oppression of the defendant—the adversary: and thus is uncovered the deep enmity which exists between him and the widow. It also tells of the severe harassment this widow has suffered at the hands of the adversary. What she complains of before the judge must undoubtedly be a rehearsal of her past experiences and of her current situation. What she asks for is that the judge may avenge her the wrongs done to her by bringing the adversary to justice.

In one sense this adversary is the central figure of the parable. Without him there would be no disturbance created under the judicial rule of the judge; nor, of course, would the widow be troubled—she could quite easily live in peace. Unquestionably, without the adversary there would be no story nor parable, for the one who stirs up all the troubles is this adversary: he is the instigator of all confusions and afflictions. And hence he ought to be the focus of our attention as we now take up the three characters in the parable one by one.

The Judge

This judge is the only authority in a certain city. He governs it *entirely*. In a sense this is a picture of the power and authority of God. Even though at present Satan temporarily rules over the world, he is but a usurper who has occupied it by force. When the Lord Jesus died on the cross He already cast out the prince of this world. In His death He "despoiled the principalities and the powers . . . [and] made a show of them openly, triumphing over them in it" (Col. 2.15). Although the world still lies under the evil one, it is totally illegal. And God has appointed a day when the kingdom shall be retaken and His Son shall be king over this world for a thousand years, and onward, then, to eternity. Yet before that time arrives God only permits Satan to remain active, while He himself holds the reins of government of this world. Satan may rule over all that belongs to Satan himself, he may even persecute all that belongs to God; nonetheless all of this is but for awhile. And even in this short while, Satan is entirely restricted by God. He may harass the saints but only within certain limits. Aside from what God permits, the enemy has no authority whatsoever. This we can perceive clearly in the story of Job. Just as this judge rules an entire city, so God rules over the entire world. And just as it is highly irregular for people under the rule of a judge to harass others and thus to become adversaries, so it is most extraordinary, even monstrous, for Satan who is under the rule of God to persecute the saints.

The character of this judge is told us in his own words: "I fear not God, nor regard man." What kind of immoral person he truly must be, neither having regard for God nor man. Yet due to the incessant coming of the widow and asking for vengeance, he is so troubled and worn out by her pleas that he finally avenges her. The Lord Jesus employs this judge in negative terms to underscore the goodness of God: for

God is not like the virtueless judge in the parable: on the contrary, He is our gracious Father and He protects us: how He always loves to give us the best of things: and He is not unrelated to us as is the judge with the widow. Now, therefore, if such a judge as this one in the parable is willing to avenge the widow because of her incessant pleading, how much more will God who is so virtuous, so kind, and so intimately related to us avenge His children who pray to Him unceasingly? If an immoral judge will avenge a woman for her continuous cry, will not God at least work because of His own people? The reason why the widow finally obtains the judge's consent to avenge her is to be found in her incessant asking. She can pin no hope in the judge himself, knowing how immoral and virtueless he is. Yet we must recognize that the answer to our prayer to God not only comes because of our praying unceasingly—which in itself should be sufficient for us to obtain what we ask for—but also because of the goodness of God. That is why the Lord Jesus concludes the parable by asking: "Shall not God avenge his elect?" These three words, "shall not God", imply a comparison. Inasmuch as the widow depends solely on her incessant asking as the means of getting what she asks for, shall we not receive that which we ask for because of our constant prayer to God and because of His goodness?

The Widow

This widow has no one on whom to rely. The very word "widow" sufficiently betrays the fact of her

isolation. The husband on whom she always depended
for her living is dead. She is now a widow. She truly
serves as a good type for us Christians in the world.
Our Lord Jesus has already ascended to heaven; so
that speaking simply from the viewpoint of the physical, Christians are as without reliance as any widow.
The teaching of Matthew 5 unveils the painful conditions of us Christians. We are to be the meekest of all,
who offer no resistance of any kind; and hence, we
suffer persecution and humiliation everywhere. The
Lord Jesus and His apostles never instruct the believers to seek for power and position in this world;
instead, they teach us to be humble and lowly by ac-
cepting the spite and harassment of this world and by
refusing to claim anything according to right or law.
Such is the position of the Christians and the path
which our Lord himself has set for us. Inasmuch as
the Son of God must die on the cross without any resistance or murmur, can His disciples ever expect a
better treatment from the world? In view of all this,
the widow here is indeed a good illustration of us
Christians in this age.

The Adversary

Now even as the widow has her adversary, so we
Christians have ours too. And our adversary is Satan.
For the very meaning of the word "Satan" is "adversary", which signifies an enemy: "your adversary the
devil" (1 Peter 5.8). We should therefore clearly recognize who is our enemy. Then we shall know how to

approach our judge who is our God and accuse our enemy. If we wish to examine the root reason for the enmity existing between us and the devil we shall find that a long history lies behind it. To put it simply, this enmity began in the garden of Eden. After the fall of man, God said: "I will put enmity between thee and the woman, and between thy seed and her seed: he shall bruise thy head, and thou shalt bruise his heel" (Gen. 3.15). Inasmuch as the devil hurt us human beings, God has placed enmity in our hearts as well as in Satan's heart.

We know that the seed of the woman mentioned here in Genesis has reference to the Lord Jesus Christ: He and the devil are eternally at enmity. And this is something appointed by God himself. We who believe in the Lord Jesus stand on the Lord's side; accordingly, we cannot but reckon the Lord's enemy to be our enemy. Likewise, Satan the enemy of our Lord will not pass us lightly by and not oppose us. He considers the Lord Jesus to be his enemy, so that he is constrained to look upon the disciples of the Lord as his enemies also. But those who have not believed in the Lord Jesus are the devil's children (see John 8.44), and naturally the devil loves his own. Yet we have believed in, and are united with, the Lord Jesus; therefore, we will incur the devil's hatred for the sake of his hate towards our Lord.

Such enmity deepens day by day. Since the enemy is so strong and we are so poor and desolate as is the widow, he uses all his powers to oppress us—causing us great loss. So much have we suffered at his hands that

we cannot stress too strongly how Christians today are
wronged by the devil. And if these wrongs are not
avenged, we will suffer loss forever. What a pity that
many of God's children are still unaware of the oppression of Satan.

Satan and the Saints

As the adversary evilly treated the widow, so the
devil today evilly treats us believers. Who knows how
much we have suffered at his hands? Of course, when
he persecutes us he neither manifests his own self nor
acts directly. All his works are done through people or
things. He is not intent upon showing forth himself; on
the contrary, he instigates people of the world to act
for him while he himself directs in secret. As the devil
took upon himself a cover in the form of a serpent at
his first working, so he will seek a cover each time he
operates today. Owing to his concealment, God's children are often mistaken in recognizing their real
enemy.

Sometimes he weakens believers' bodies, causing
sickness and pain (see Acts 10.38); yet the believers
may regard their conditions in terms only of hygiene
or fatigue, without realizing that the devil is at work
behind the scenes. In this one respect alone, oh how
greatly do the Christians suffer at his hands!

Sometimes the enemy incites people of this world
to persecute believers (see Rev. 2.10), who are therefore attacked by their communities, friends, and family members. Yet they think this is due to people's ha-

tred towards the Lord; what they do not perceive is that the devil actually instigates the assaults.

Sometimes the evil one works in the environment, involving believers in hardships and dangers. Frequently he will create misunderstanding among Christians so as to separate the dearest of friends and cause much heartbreak and tears.

Sometimes the enemy cuts off believers' material supplies, reducing them to wants and even to starvation. At still other times he oppresses their spirit and makes them feel depressed, restless and aimless. Or he may afflict the will of believers, causing them to lose the power of free choice and thus not be able to know what to do. Or he injects irrational fear into believers' hearts. Or Satan heaps things upon them to overtire them, or else takes away sleep from them to wear them out. Or he injects unclean or confused thoughts into their mind to weaken their resistance or else fashions himself into an angel of light to deceive and to lead the believers astray.

It is just impossible to exhaust the list of all the works the devil does. In short, the enemy will do anything which can cause believers to suffer either spiritually or physically, to fall into sins, or to incur loss or damage. Unfortunately, many of God's children are unaware of the works of Satan when they suffer at his hands. Whatever happens they attribute to the natural, the accidental, and the human—not discerning how in many natural occurrences there abides the satanically supernatural, how in many accidental episodes there hides the devilish plotting, and how in many human dealings there is involved the wicked maneuvers of the enemy.

Identify the Enemy

The most important thing before us now is to identify the enemy. We should know for sure who is our adversary, who it is that causes us much suffering. How frequently we account our sufferings to be from men. But the Bible tells us that "our wrestling is not against flesh and blood, but against the principalities, against the powers, against the worldrulers of this darkness, against the spiritual hosts of wickedness in the heavenly places" (Eph. 6.12). Hence every time we suffer from the hand of man, we need to remember that behind flesh and blood Satan and his powers of darkness can very well be there directing everything. We should have the necessary spiritual insight to discern the work of God from the maneuver of Satan at the back of everything. We should distinguish what is natural and what is supernatural. We should be so inwardly exercised as to gain knowledge of the spiritual realm so that none of Satan's hidden work can escape our observation.

Such being the case, shall we not recognize that what we usually consider to be incidental and natural happenings may involve the works of the enemy behind the scenes? We shall readily see that Satan is really trying to frustrate us at every turn and oppress us in all things. What a pity we have suffered so much from him in the past without knowing that it was he who made us suffer. Now part of the most urgent work of ours today is to generate a heart of hatred towards Satan for his cruelty. We do not need to be fearful lest our enmity towards Satan becomes too deep. Before there is the possibility of our overcoming we must maintain in our heart a hostile attitude towards him, no longer willing to subject ourselves to his oppression. We ought to understand that what we have suffered at Satan's hands is a real grievance which must be avenged. He has no right to harass us, yet he does it anyway. This is indeed an injustice, a grievance which cannot remain unavenged.

The Cry for Vindication

Now after this widow has suffered much, she comes to the judge asking for justice. This is something we ought to learn to do. We do not come to earthly judges, imploring them to act for us. No, we ask our judge who is none other than our Father God in heaven. The weapons of our warfare are not of the flesh (2 Cor. 10.4), therefore we will not employ any earthly or fleshly means against the instruments of flesh and blood utilized by Satan. Quite the contrary, instead of showing impatience, anger or even hostility towards them, we should pity them for they are but the instruments of Satan. Let us see that in spiritual warfare the weapons of flesh are utterly useless. They are not only useless, but whoever uses them will without fail be overcome by Satan.

Spiritual weapons are of many kinds as we find recorded in Ephesians 6. The most effective among these weapons is prayer, mentioned in verse 18. True, we are without strength and therefore unable to avenge ourselves of our adversary. Yet we may pray to our God, asking him to avenge us. Prayer is the best offensive weapon against our enemy. Through it we may preserve our line of defense intact. Through prayer we can also attack our enemy and inflict great loss on his plan, work, and power. This widow realized that if she struggled with her adversary by herself she would not prevail because she, being a weak widow, could never withstand a powerful rogue such as he. In the same way, if God's children strive independently without relying, by means of prayer, on God's power and backing to accuse the enemy and to ask God for vindication, they too will be injured by fiery darts. In this parable the Lord Jesus teaches us the best way to overcome the adversary, which is to pray day and night to God—asking Him to avenge us of our enemy by judging him.

Prayer That Resists Satan

The Bible gives us many helps in this matter of praying against Satan. We will here examine a few of these passages so as to learn how to offer up such prayer.

We recall how in Genesis 3 God punished and cursed the devil after his first evil working. In that divine curse God plainly foretold that the head of the devil would be crushed by the Lord Jesus at the cross. Accordingly, whenever we suffer under the devil's hands we may take advantage of the punishment meted out to him by praying: "O God, curse Satan afresh so that he cannot do what he pleases. You have crushed him in the garden of Eden. I ask You to curse him anew, placing him again under the power of the cross so as to immobilize him." What the devil fears most is the curse of God. As soon as God curses, Satan dare not hurt us.

It is recorded in Mark 1 that when the Lord Jesus cast out demons He did not permit them to speak. Hence when Satan uses people to utter many words of misunderstanding or violence, we may ask the Lord to shut his mouth and not permit him to speak through them. Sometimes as we are preaching the gospel or teaching people, we may ask the Lord to forbid the devil to speak to our audience so as to induce them to doubt or to resist the word of God. We remember the story of Daniel in the lions' den. One prayer is really quite effective: "O Lord, shut the lion's mouth; do not allow him to hurt Your own people."

Matthew 12 furnishes us with another good word on prayer from the Lord: "How can one enter into the house of the strong man, and spoil his goods, except he first bind the strong man? and then he will spoil his house" (v.29). We know that the strong man to whom the Lord refers is Satan. In order to overcome Satan we must first bind him, thus immobilizing him. We ourselves, of course, do not have the strength to bind the strong man and cause him to lose his freedom in resisting our works. But we can pray. In our prayer we may ask God to bind Satan and render him powerless.

Each time we begin a work, if we first bind Satan in prayer our victory is assured. We ought always to pray: "O Lord, bind the strong man."

"To this end was the Son of God manifested, that he might destroy the works of the devil" (1 John 3.8). As soon as we discern a work of the devil, we can pray as follows: "O God, Your Son was manifested to destroy the works of the devil. How we thank You, for He has destroyed the devil's works on the cross. But the devil is now again working. Please destroy his work in us, destroy his manipulation over our work, destroy his devices in our environment, and destroy all his works." When we pray, we may pray according to the current situation in which we find ourselves. If we notice that Satan is working in us or family or work or school or nation, we can ask God to destroy his work in that particular area.

Jude records the word which Michael the archangel declared to Satan: "The Lord rebuke thee" (v.9). After that word was spoken Satan did not dare resist anymore. We may therefore use this same word in our prayer against him. We ask the Lord to rebuke the enemy. We ought to know that the Lord hearkens to such prayer. If we ask Him to rebuke, He will rebuke. We must also believe that after the Lord has rebuked Satan, the enemy is no longer able to withstand, for he is afraid of the Lord's rebuke. When our Lord rebuked the wind and the sea, these elements listened to Him and instantly the wind ceased and the sea became calm. His rebuke produces the same effect on Satan.

In reading the Psalms we will see how effective is the rebuke of the Lord! "Then the channels of water appeared, and the foundations of the world were laid bare, at thy rebuke, O Jehovah, at the blast of the breath of thy nostrils" (18.15). "At thy rebuke, O God of Jacob, both chariot and horse are cast into a dead sleep" (76.6). "It is burned with fire, it is cut down: they perish at the rebuke of thy countenance" (80.16). "At thy rebuke they fled; at the voice of thy thunder they hasted away" (104.7). "He rebuked the Red Sea also, and it was dried up" (106.9). These Scripture verses show us the power of the rebuke of the Lord. If the Lord rebukes Satan, the latter can never withstand. When the enemy oppresses us, we should ask God to rebuke him.

It is written in Matthew 16 that for the sake of human affection Peter wished to block the Lord Jesus from going to the cross. The Lord rebuked him, saying, "Get thee behind me, Satan" (v.23). Whenever the devil makes use of our friends or relatives to hinder us—for the sake of human affection—from doing God's will, we may ask God to put Satan behind us.

In Matthew 6 it is recorded that the Lord Jesus teaches us to pray in this fashion: "Deliver us from the evil one" (v.13). Since we do not know when the evil one will come to molest us, we ought to pray with this word.

Our Lord Jesus, "having despoiled the principalities and the powers, . . . made a show of them openly, triumphing over them in it [the cross]" (Col. 2.15). Whenever we see the devil's power on a rampage we should stand on the ground of the cross, asking the

Lord to put the devil to shame once more. The devil has already suffered shame on the cross; so, based on his first humiliation, we can ask the Lord to put him to shame again. When the devil is shamed, he dare not raise his head. How then can he molest us again? Hence let us pray: "O Lord, we now stand on the foundation of the cross, asking You to again put the devil to shame."

The Duration of Prayer

How long ought we to pray such prayer? We know there are many prayers which need to be prayed only once. But prayer which attacks Satan has no fear of being too much. The purpose of this parable which our Lord gives is that we "ought *always* to pray" (Luke 18.1). This judge avenges the widow not for the sake of justice nor for any other reason but because he cannot stand her continual coming. Does he not say to himself, "I will avenge her, lest she wear me out by her continual coming"? Consequently, this kind of prayer should be offered without intermission. Such prayer against the adversary is not merely to be uttered at times of special need, it is to be maintained as an attitude and breathed unceasingly in the spirit in ordinary days when all is calm. The Lord Jesus, in explaining the word of this parable, asks: "And shall not God avenge his elect, that cry to him day and night"? This kind of prayer must therefore be prayed day and night without ceasing. We should accuse our enemy before God incessantly, since we are told in Revelation 12 that Satan "accuseth [the brethren] before our God day and night" (v.10). If he accuses us day and night, should we not also accuse him day and night?

This is true vindication: as the devil treats us, so shall we treat him. The cry of this widow continued on until the adversary was judged and punished and she was avenged of her grievance. As long as there is another day in which Satan still usurps the world, and so long as he is not yet imprisoned in the bottomless pit or cast into the lake of fire, we will not cease from praying against him. Not until God has avenged us and Satan has in truth fallen as lightning from heaven shall our prayer come to an end. How much it is the desire of God that we show deeper hatred towards the devil. Have we not suffered enough from him?!? He has shown his enmity towards us at every step of our way, he has caused us to suffer terribly both in body and in spirit; why, then, do we endure his persecution without speech or prayer? Why have we not risen up to accuse him before our God with words of prayer? We ought to seek for vindication. Why do we not continually approach God and accuse the enemy, thus releasing the long-suppressed exasperation? The Lord Jesus is calling us today to oppose the devil with prayer.

The Effect of Prayer

What is the effect of such prayer? Its effect is seen at two different times. First is the immediate effect. Every time the enemy is accused he is once again restricted by God from hurting us. Though after a lapse of time he may return, nonetheless during the period in which he is being accused, he does not dare do any violence; for each time we claim the victory of the cross, that victory becomes real to us once more. Every time we pray against the enemy, his work is again destroyed by the Lord and he himself is rebuked afresh by the Lord. If we pray one more time Satan will suffer one more loss. As God hears our prayer one more time, the profit of Satan is despoiled one more time.

Yet this effect goes beyond the immediate. The Lord Jesus lays stress here on the *ultimate* vindication. As we pray time and again, the Lord rebukes and destroys the devil again and again. But this is not yet final, that is, it is not once and for all; because the devil is only temporarily restricted; he has still to suffer the consequence of his final defeat. "And shall not God avenge his elect, that cry to him day and night," asks the Lord, "and yet he is long-suffering over them." This refers to Satan's ultimate destruction. We know how the enemy will be imprisoned in the bottomless pit during the millennial kingdom. Afterwards he will be cast by the Lord Jesus into the lake of fire. Then is the ultimate vindication of the believers. For this reason, Christians today ought to offer up much prayer against the devil, in order that their grievances might be forever vindicated. Now is the time of the long-suffering of God. Even though He does hear believers' prayers and restricts the works of the devil, He nevertheless has not wholly cast the devil out to make it impossible for him to molest us.

Hence this is also the time for believers to pray in order to hasten the dawning of that day. In this respect, our prayer would seem to have the effect of accelerating God's working. If the widow did not always plead, who would have known when the judge would have ever avenged her of her adversary. Her constant pleading speeded up the day of her vindication. We today must do likewise. "I say unto you," says the Lord, "that he will avenge them speedily." It would appear as if the Lord is here implying that the speed of God's work is determined by the frequency of our prayer. If we always accuse the devil in prayer, God will avenge us speedily. When the Lord Jesus comes again, He will cast Satan out of heaven so as to deprive him of all his power. Prayer which accuses Satan will hasten the day of the Lord's return.

Work Together with God

We often reflect that God does all things according to His will. This is doubtless correct. However, it is only one side of the truth, not the whole truth. God works according to His will—that is surely His principle; but when He really gets to working He always waits for His children to express their sympathy with His will through prayer before He does anything.

How God needs men to work together with Him. He truly has His own will, yet He wants men to ask according to His will. Then He will quickly accomplish the work of His determinate will. Without the prayer of His children, which indicates their working together with Him, He will not perform alone what He wills to do. To destroy the devil is God's intention. To avenge the believers is undoubtedly His will. Nevertheless, He waits for His children's prayers. Just as the judge in the parable would not have avenged the widow if she had not come and pleaded her cause, so God today will not avenge the believers speedily if they do not pray against Satan. We do not know exactly why this is so, and yet we do know how much God likes His people to work together with Him. Naturally, accusation must be based on fact. But as believers are indisputably being harrassed by Satan, they may accuse him before God of the ill-treatment they have received. And this will put him to death.

The Last Days

When the Lord Jesus finished speaking this parable, He concluded with a final word: "Nevertheless, when the Son of man cometh, shall he find faith on the earth?" Judging by this statement, it would seem as though at the time of His soon return, there will be a great lack of this kind of prayer among His own people. They do not pray such prayer because they have no faith. They speculate that it is too big and too difficult a thing to cast Satan from heaven into the bottomless pit and then the lake of fire. Since the promise that "the God of peace shall bruise Satan under your feet shortly" (Rom. 16.20) has yet to be fulfilled after twenty centuries, how can I expect God to finish off Satan through my prayer? What the Lord Jesus means by His word is that at the time of His imminent return people will lack faith in praying about this matter. However, the last days is the time when we should so pray. Can we be the few faithful ones who, in the days when such prayer is so rare, offer up prayers against the devil so as to cause him to lose position and power? We know in the last days Satan and his evil spirits are to be exceptionally active in their operations. Therefore, we must pray more than ever against him and overthrow his government. Speaking truthfully, there is no greater work which God's children could do today than this work. Who is willing to pray against Satan for the sake of God and himself?

"Strive thou, O Jehovah, with them that strive with me: fight thou against them that fight against me. Take hold of shield and buckler, and stand up for my help. Draw out also the spear, and stop the way against them that pursue me: say unto my soul, I am thy salvation. Let them be put to shame and brought to dishonor that seek after my soul: let them be turned back and confounded that devise my hurt. Let them be as chaff before the wind, and the angel of Jehovah driving them on. Let their way be dark and slippery, and the angel of Jehovah pursuing them. For without cause have they hid for me their net in a pit; without cause have they digged a pit for my soul. . . . Stir up thyself, and awake to the justice due unto me, even unto my cause, my God and my Lord" (Ps. 35.1–7,23).

6 | Some Pointers on Prayer

First, Has God given us sufficient provision for prayer? Yes, God has given us sufficient provision in His Son by the Holy Spirit. Without such adequate provision we might draw back from our privilege and duty of prayer. But thank the Lord, He has provided us with all the right conditions for drawing nigh to Him and living before Him. We may sum up His provision in two words: trust and help.

Let us consider "trust" first. Trust means having the ability to entrust to, boldness to rely on, the full assurance to depend upon, and so forth. It really includes a very great deal. A spirit of trust is most essential to prayer and to the total Christian life. If our relationship with the Lord continually fluctuates—with our having neither assurance nor confidence— our entire life will be fatally wounded. Let us look at the following passages from the Bible:

"Having therefore, brethren, boldness to enter into the holy place by the blood of Jesus, by the way which he dedicated for us, a new and living way, . . . and having a great priest; . . . let us draw near with a true heart in fulness of faith . . ." (Heb. 10.19–22). "Through whom also we have had our access by faith into this grace wherein we stand" (Rom. 5.2). "For through him we both have our access in one Spirit unto the Father" (Eph. 2.18). "In whom we have boldness and access in confidence through our faith in him" (Eph. 3.12).

True trust is based on one factor, which is Christ himself. We have absolute privilege to draw near to God because Christ himself is that privilege which we have. This is God's provision. In Christ's name we may come to the Father at any time anywhere. We never approach the Father in our name or our condition because this is simply impossible. We come to see the Father in the name of the Son alone.

It is stated in Ephesians 3.12 that in Christ Jesus our Lord we have boldness and access in confidence through our faith in Him. We do not come to God by bringing our "unworthiness" to Him; rather, it is Christ who takes our hand and leads us to the Father. He introduces into the presence of God all who are cleansed by the blood as those who have been raised from the dead, for we are clothed with "Him" as our robe of righteousness. Hence our trust is Christ himself.

Next, let us consider the term "help". Blessed are those who can draw near to God with boldness and confidence! Possessing such a high privilege, we nevertheless sense so much of our own inability, weakness and foolishness that we do not know how to pray. How good it can be if we know and experience the help of the Holy Spirit here.

"And in like manner the Spirit also helpeth our infirmity: for we know not how to pray as we ought; but the Spirit himself maketh intercession for us with groanings which cannot be uttered; and he that searcheth the hearts knoweth what is the mind of the Spirit, because he maketh intercession for the saints according to the will of God" (Rom. 8.26,27). Our weakness is most easily manifested in prayer. Nothing in the spiritual realm reveals our weakness more than this activity. We all are aware of the great difficulty the disciples experienced in prayer in the garden of Gethsemane. They could not watch and pray. Yet, thank God, we have the almighty Holy Spirit to help us. We must rely on the indwelling Holy Spirit, who works within us with might, for He is our help in times of infirmity and ignorance. Though we do not know how to pray, even so, the indwelling Holy Spirit who himself knows the will of God, will teach us to pray according to the mind of God. Moreover, He will give meaning to our fellowship with God and will thus lead us into the reality of communion. When we pray, therefore, let us depend on the Christ whom we believe and the Holy Spirit who is our help.

Second, Why does Satan try to resist prayer? Satan is determined to cut off our communion with heaven; consequently, he is willing to pay any price to hinder true prayer. Let us ever be aware of the fact that he persistently attacks the prayers of the church as well as of the believers. If he succeeds in an attack on prayer he knows he can rest in peace. We must therefore be watchful and on guard against the enemy, especially when we are going to pray.

In dealing with Satanic attack we should pay particular attention to the following areas:

(1) Satan will attack our trust in the Lord. He knows if he can make us feel unworthy, unable, and that we are losing trust in the Lord, he will take away our heart to pray.

(2) Sometimes he also attacks our body, even our thoughts, nerves, or other facets related to our body. When we feel tired—and without strength—we do not like to pray. Let us guard against these and overcome them. As to the rest of the things which are beyond our control, the Lord will be responsible.

(3) Sometimes the devil will attack our appointed time of prayer, both private and in the church. Many have experienced this. How subtle is the enemy. If he cannot succeed in having our time of prayer fully occupied with other things, he will see to it that we do not have real prayer at that time. Frequently we are able to maintain the time of prayer, but we lack the life of prayer.

(4) Sometimes Satan attacks our constant fellowship with the Lord by creating a heavy obstructive layer between us and our Lord so that we cannot make contact. It appears as though a mysterious mist separates us from the Lord.

(5) Finally, he purposes to push us into darkness so that we cannot see the necessity of prayer. He will constantly distract our attention towards other things, thus hurting our prayer life. May we never fall into his trap. We ought to look to the Lord, gather many materials for prayer, and pay much attention to God's interests and needs. Our responsibility in prayer is not a small matter—let us therefore watch and pray.

Third, Aside from personal prayer, what other kind of prayer must we attend to, in accordance with the word of God? We must have corporate prayer, which is the prayer of the church.

When we talk about the prayer of the church we are no less concerned with private prayer nor sense any less the importance of personal prayer. Yet let us see that it is a rule in the kingdom of God that what one person is unable to do in certain respects is to be done through mutual and corporate help. Especially in the matter of prayer, there is the need for mutuality. All who follow the Lord closely frequently see the need of praying with other believers. At times they feel the inadequacy of their own prayer. Particularly in praying for such a colossal subject as the kingdom of God, it requires the strength of the whole church. "My house," says the Lord, "shall be called a house of prayer" (Matt. 21.13). To this we may add, "whose house are we" (Heb. 3.6).

"Again I say unto you," declares the Lord, "that if two of you shall agree on earth as touching anything

that they shall ask, it shall be done for them of my
Father who is in heaven. For where two or three are
gathered together in my name, there am I in the midst
of them" (Matt. 18.19,20). Both fact and experience
tell us that the portion of Christ is greater in the gathering of believers in the name of the Lord than in each
individual, for the Lord is in the midst of the church
whereas He cannot be in the midst of an individual
(there is no "in the midst of " to an individual because
the Lord is in the individual. That portion of Christ in
the midst is what one person cannot have, individu-
ally). When we are truly gathered together in the
Lord, how much more we sense the broadness of an
horizon in prayer, how greatly strengthened we are in
prayer warfare. Furthermore, we often experience in a
prayer meeting the revelation of God's mind to us
through the Holy Spirit giving us burden as well as ut-
terance in prayer. No doubt there are many things we
may say about the prayer of the church*, but perhaps
we ought to stop here and simply say one important
word: that the prayer of the church can never be a
substitute to private prayer, although at the same time
it should be noted that personal prayer is continually
falling behind the prayer of the church and can never
catch up with it.

Fourth, What are the various aspects in the work

---

*For more information on this subject please consult: Watchman
Nee, *The Prayer Ministry of the Church* (New York: Christian
Fellowship Publishers, 1973), translated from the Chinese.

of prayer which need attention? Quite a few things require our attention in the work of prayer, among them being the following:

(1) Fellowship with the Lord in all things. We ought to bring all things in our life to the Lord, for there is nothing common or insignificant in the Christian life. To fellowship with the Lord in all things should be our daily natural habit (see Phil. 4.6).

(2) Ask and keep on asking, for the Lord delights in people asking Him. He is the rich Giver; therefore He wants men to ask. "If any of you lacketh . . . , let him ask of God, who giveth to all liberally and upbraideth not; and it shall be given him. But let him ask in faith, nothing doubting" (James 1.5,6). "Ye have not, because ye ask not. Ye ask, and receive not, because ye ask amiss" (James 4.2,3). Asking includes trust and desire. If the motive of our asking is pure, there is nothing better.

(3) Meditate and intercede. We stand before the Lord to pray for other people. Actually this is fellowship with the Lord in His high-priestly function. How He himself intercedes unceasingly for His people and their needs (Heb. 7.25; cf. Col. 4.12).

(4) Pray always. In speaking of praying with importunity we need first of all to get rid of an improper concept which holds that our God is very reluctant to answer prayer. To pray with persistency simply means that, having clearly recognized God's need, you keep on praying. Why does the Lord not answer immediately? Why should the days of His silence be prolonged? Here are at least two reasons: (a) that God

needs a full reaction from His people concerning the thing with which He is concerned and in which He is deeply interested; and (b) that sometimes such constant prayer is necessary due to a certain kind of need or environment—because of the strongholds which Satan builds, more intensified prayer is required to destroy them (see Matt. 7.7,8; Mark 9.28,29).

(5) Executive prayer. As we are united with the Lord who sits on the throne (for He is Lord of all), we may pray in His name which is above all names (Phil. 2.9).

(6) Prayer warfare. Through prayer we uplift the victory of the cross in dealing with all things. The movement of prayer follows the victory of the Lord (see Eph. 6.10–20).

(7) The prayer of faith. Under certain circumstances the Holy Spirit imparts to us a kind of inward assurance, causing us to know the will of God. Thus we will see our prayer instantly assured (see Acts 9.40).

(8) Prayer burden. Prayer is a kind of travail in spiritual birth, which is an entering into fellowhip with the sufferings of Christ, with the heart of the Father, and with the groanings of the Holy Spirit— until the day of glory (see Gal. 4.19).

Fifth, What is the central objective of prayer? God desires to have a glorious church. The central purpose of prayer is to prepare for Christ a glorious church that is conformed to Him. This is the revelation of the entire Bible. It is the central thought of God. We need to pay special attention to it, for it is the desire of the Lord himself as well. Before He was crucified, He expressed this thought in His great intercessory prayer recorded in John 17. In the epistles of Paul this heart desire is also most evident. This is not to suggest, however, that there is to be a reducing of prayers for other things. It only serves to give a central focus to all kinds of prayer offered up. Having this objective in mind, our other prayers will be lifted up to a higher level. If we see that the preaching of the gospel is more than causing people to come out of death into life but also and more centrally to bring men into an eternal, wonderful union with the glorious Christ, then our intercessory prayer for the world can only increase and not decrease. Furthermore, a great need today is to let the world see the glory of Christ through His church. By the power of the Holy Spirit the church ought to impress the world with the fact that she is indeed the channel of blessing to the world.

Finally, it is the determinate will of God that we should have more intelligent and intimate communion with Him. He wants us—His many sons—to come to Him in His beloved Son our Lord Jesus Christ. He desires many priests to accompany the one great High Priest (He who "ever lives to make intercession for them"—Heb. 7.25) in the work of intercession. "He made us to be a kingdom, to be priests unto his God and Father" (Rev. 1.6). "But ye are . . . a royal priesthood" (1 Peter 2.9).

7 | The Wearing-Out Tactics of Satan

*And he shall speak words against the Most High, and
shall wear out the saints of the Most High. (Dan. 7.25)*

Satan has a work, which is attacking the children
of God. His attack may not come suddenly; oftentimes, it comes gradually and slowly. Daniel 7.25
mentions how Satan shall wear out the saints of the
Most High. Satan has in fact a plan against the saints
of the Most High, which is to wear them out. Hence
let us clearly recognize that the work of Satan in the
lives of God's children is frequently not very notice-
able, since his work is slowly to wear them down.

What is the meaning of the phrase, "wear out"? It
has in it the idea of reducing a little this minute, then
reducing a little further the next minute. Reduce a little today and reduce a little more tomorrow. Thus the
wearing out is almost imperceptible; nevertheless, it *is*
a reducing. The wearing down is scarcely an activity

of which one is conscious, yet the end result is that there is nothing left. Hence this principle of Satan's working in the lives of God's children is to wear them out until they are worn down completely. He will wear you out a little today and then a little more the next day. He will make you suffer a small amount now and a little more later. You may think this to be something insignificant, nevertheless Satan knows that the consequence of such wearing away is to wear the saint out completely.

For this reason, the Bible indicates that "the love of the many shall wax cold" (Matt. 24.12), which means a *gradually* growing cold. It also mentions how a certain maid, having a spirit of divination, cried out after Paul and his colleagues for *many days* (see Acts 16.17–18). Moreover, the Scriptures record that when Felix hoped that Paul would give him money, he sent for Paul the *oftener* and communed with him (Acts 24.26). And the Old Testament also describes how Delilah pressed Samson *daily* with her word and so urged him continually that his soul was vexed unto death (Judges 16.16). Such is how Satan gradually, and for many days, will frequently wear out the children of God. "The evil day" spoken of in Ephesians 6.13 refers to the wearing-out tactics of Satan. We must ask God to open our eyes that we may discern how Satan would wear us out and how we should combat his wearing-out tactic.

Wearing Out the Physical Body

Especially with respect to the human body, we

may easily see how the enemy wears out the children of God. Two examples come to mind: the smiting of Job's body (Job 2.7,8) and the thorn in Paul's flesh (2 Cor. 12.7). These are classic cases of Satan's wearing out men's bodies. Quite a few Christians experience sickness and the weakening of their body after they are saved, whereas formerly they were rather healthy. Should the Lord open our eyes we will perceive that there is one who is scheming against the children of God all the time, and that one is Satan. Along this same line, we ought to point out how many of the Lord's servants, before they went forth to preach the gospel, were in good health, but that after they went out to work for the Lord their health failed in a short period of three to five years. This is the enemy wearing out the saints of the Most High. He makes the child of God eat a little less today and sleep a little less tomorrow. He causes him to feel a little tired today and a little more tired tomorrow. By thus adding a little at a time, a believer's health can finally become entirely shaken. Such is the work of Satan.

Wearing Out Man's Heart

Not only does he work on the body, Satan also works in the human heart. Upon first believing in the Lord you may feel very happy, joyful and peaceful. But if you are not watchful—being ignorant of what the enemy can do—you will find yourself one day mysteriously uncomfortable. You feel somewhat restless today, somewhat unhappy tomorrow, and somewhat depressed the day after. Little by little, your peace is completely lost, your joy totally gone. This is the way the devil wears you down to a state of fatigue and despair.

Wearing Out the Spiritual Life

Satan also wears out your spiritual life. He will take away your prayer life little by little, and cause you to trust God less and less and yourself more and more, a little at a time. He will make you feel somewhat cleverer than before. Step by step you are misled to rely more on your own gift, and step by step your heart is enticed away from the Lord. Now were Satan to strike the children of God with great force at one time, they would know how to resist the enemy since they would immediately recognize his work. What is so wickedly subtle about Satan, though, is that he does not strike with one grand stroke; instead, he will employ the tactic of wearing out the saints over an extended period of time, thus causing God's children to lose out and to backslide a little at a time. He uses this method of gradualism to wear down the people of God.

Wearing Out Our Time

Satan will also wear out our time. Felix often sent for Paul and communed with him. After two years of conversation with the powerful and gifted apostle, he was still unsaved. This is the enemy's device to wear people out. Today, Paul is invited to talk without any result; tomorrow he is again invited to talk, with still no result; and the day afterwards he is once more invited to talk, and again, without any result. Paul was inveigled to engage in "resultless" work for two whole years. How the enemy wears out man's time and energy!

If the children of God do not discern Satan's wiles they can easily fall into his trap. How we must redeem our time and make every hour count. We must resist Satan from wearing out our time and must withstand him from causing us to do works that will have no results.

Wearing Out Samson's Consecration

Samson had failures, but he should not have lost his consecration nor his testimony of separation. For the loss of consecration means the loss of power, and the loss of testimony signifies the loss of the presence of God. Samson was a Nazarite, one who was consecrated to God. Satan knew that the source of this man's power lay in his consecration. Hence in order to touch Samson's lifespring, he must take away his consecration. How did he do it? He used the woman Delilah, who "pressed [Samson] daily with her words, and urged him, that his soul was vexed unto death. And he told her all his heart" (Judges 16.16,17). Thus did Samson reveal the secret of his power. And subsequently, he fell into the snare of Satan: he lost his consecration, power, testimony of separation and the presence of God. Such "pressing daily" is done by the enemy.

If our eyes are opened by God we shall be able to see that when Satan wears people out he employs all kinds of ways. He wears out the body, men's heart, and one's spiritual life. He does not attack violently; he wears out slowly. We must therefore guard against the wearing-out tactics of Satan. We must not let him wear us down. We will instead resist him at every step.

Must Detest the Wearing Out Work of Satan

When Paul was preaching in Macedonia he met a certain maid having a spirit of divination. She followed after him and cried out, saying, "These men are servants of the Most High God, who proclaim unto you the way of salvation." And this she did for many days until Paul was so sorely troubled that he turned and declared to the spirit, "I charge thee in the name of Jesus Christ to come out of her." And the evil spirit came out that very moment (see Acts 16.16–18). In the spiritual realm we need to have such detestation as Paul exhibited here. We are not to detest men but must detest the evil spirits. Paul, for sure, loathed the evil spirit but not the maid. He commanded the spirit to come out of her. In the affair, he treated the maid as a third person. Let us have Paul's kind of detestation whenever the devil is wearing men down.

If you really know how Satan tries to wear you out, you will ask God to give you this sense of detestation—which is, to loathe Satan and be angry with him!

Many know how to lose their temper on men but strangely enough do not know how to hurl their temper on Satan. When they are annoyed by people they will be thrown into a fit of temper, yet they are not aware of how the enemy is wearing them down. Day after day Paul was being worn down by Satan until he was so exasperated that he opened his mouth to resist the evil spirit, and thus the spirit left the maid. Hence do not keep silent all the time. Let there be voice raised in resistance. If God's children would grow angry and open their mouths to oppose Satan, all would be well. If people will become angry with the devil we will shout Hallelujah, How wonderful! How very pitiful are some, who are so weak that they allow the enemy to wear them down all the time. Children of God should be angry at Satan and should detest him. By being angry and showing abhorrence they cease experiencing the wearing down of the enemy.

How frequently as you are being worn down by Satan you keep silent, patiently enduring and quietly suffering until you feel so disgusted within yourself and become so angry that you declare: "I oppose this, I will not have it!" Just by saying this, just by being infuriated about it, you are delivered and the wearing out process ends. God's children should therefore rise up to repudiate and reprove the enemy. Some people fail to get relieved because they still have "strength" to endure. A person who keeps on enduring Satanic wear and tear, allowing the devil to waste away his energy, his joy and his spiritual life, has fallen into the wile of the enemy. Let us be clear, of course, that we should not be angry at the people who are used by Satan; on the contrary, we ought to be patient with them, even loving them. But we must oppose and resist the hidden conspiracy of Satan. If we withstand what he does, we will soon be freed.

The power to resist the evil one comes from discerning his pressure. A number of believers, when they are manipulated and assaulted, do withstand and resist him; yet they find no strength in themselves. This is because they fail to see Satan's pressure. Though they resist, they do not seem to have the strength to raise their voice against the enemy. Whether or not you can resist him depends on how much you detest him. If you are not quite annoyed at him, your words to him will vanish into the air. But if you are really exasperated, you become angry at him. This anger becomes your power. As you open your mouth you cause him to flee.

Such a detestation comes from revelation. Because you perceive how the devil keeps on wearing you down, you resist him. The moment you see this, Satan knows his tactic is discovered and his hope is lost. May God truly have mercy upon us that we may recognize the wearing-out work of Satan. Let us realize that if we patiently endure, the work of Satan will most certainly continue; but if we are outraged, he will immediately leave us alone. Let us understand that all means of resistance are of no avail except we speak out to resist, and then we shall see that Satan is forced to retreat. If one day we recognize what Satan is doing—that he does plan everything—we shall rise up boldly and declare: "I reject it; I oppose it!" And as God gives us such a resistance, it instantly becomes effective.

In conclusion, we ought to read Ephesians 6.13, in which Paul writes that we, "having done all" ought "to stand"; we must stand, and not allow Satan to continue wearing us down. We should ask the Lord to open our eyes to see what wearing-out work Satan is performing on the children of God. May we rise up to resist and to speak against the enemy. May we declare: "I resist, I oppose, I do not accept such wearing down." If we reject and resist whatever wearing-down tactic Satan may use upon us, we shall witness the salvation of the Lord and the deliverance from Satan's wearing-out strategem.

Such a word needs the covering of the blood. May God cover us with the blood.